of related interest

The Healthy Coping Colouring Book and Journal
Creative Activities to Help Manage Stress, Anxiety and Other Big Feelings
Pooky Knightsmith
Illustrated by Emily Hamilton
ISBN 978 1 78592 139 1
eISBN 978 1 78450 405 2

Trans Teen Survival Guide
Owl Fisher and Fox Fisher
ISBN 978 1 78592 341 8
eISBN 978 1 78450 662 9

How to Understand Your Gender
A Practical Guide for Exploring Who You Are
Alex Iantaffi and Meg-John Barker
Foreword by S. Bear Bergman
ISBN 978 1 78592 746 1
eISBN 978 1 78450 517 2

The Reflective Workbook for Partners of Transgender People
Your Transition as Your Partner Transitions
D. M. Maynard
ISBN 978 1 78592 772 0
eISBN 978 1 78450 672 8

Trans Love
An Anthology of Transgender and Non-Binary Voices
Edited by Freiya Benson
ISBN 978 1 78592 432 3
eISBN 978 1 78450 804 3

the Trans Self-Care Workbook

A Coloring Book and Journal for
Trans and Non-Binary People

Theo Nicole Lorenz

Jessica Kingsley Publishers
London and Philadelphia

First published in Great Britain in 2021 by Jessica Kingsley Publishers
An Hachette Company

4

Trigger Warning: This book mentions suicide, abuse, and cyberbullying.

A CIP catalogue record for this title is available from the British Library and the Library of Congress

ISBN 978 1 78775 343 3
eISBN 978 1 78775 344 0

Printed and bound by CPI Group (UK) Ltd, Croydon, CR0 4YY

Jessica Kingsley Publishers' policy is to use papers that are natural, renewable, and recyclable products and made from wood grown in sustainable forests. The logging and manufacturing processes are expected to conform to the environmental regulations of the country of origin.

Jessica Kingsley Publishers
73 Collier Street
London N1 9BE, UK

www.jkp.com

Contents

Introduction

Hi, my name is Theo, and my pronouns are they/them. I am your tour guide through this book, but I am not the expert—you are. No one knows your gender identity like you do. What I am is a fellow trans person who spent too many years feeling pained and alone because I thought that was how trans people were supposed to feel.

Spoiler: It's not.

We all know the culturally approved trans narrative: A trans person knows from three years old that they were "born in the wrong body," faces decades of silent agony before coming out, takes X medication and has Y and Z surgeries, and finally becomes a member of the opposite sex. Usually when you see this narrative in the media, the trans person's defining personality trait is their transness, and their only hobby is gender-related woe.

That narrative doesn't reflect all of us. It doesn't even reflect *most* of us.

I've known trans folks who spent decades in denial and doubt before they came out, and I've known trans folks for whom the realization was relatively quick and painless. One person I know realized and came to terms with their gender identity over the course of about five minutes, an "Oh, that's me" moment in the middle of a conversation. (Was I scathingly jealous to hear about this? Yes. Do I respect the hell out of their journey? Also yes.)

I've known people who considered themselves fully transitioned with medication but no surgery, surgery but no medication, and no medical intervention at all. I've known trans activists, trans people who considered their gender to be the least interesting thing about them, trans people living with and without a big trans community. I've known binary trans people, non-binary trans people, genderfluid and agender and a couple dozen other varieties of people whose labels are all different ways of saying "My gender is not what was written on my birth certificate."

Personally, I identify as trans and non-binary. It took me a lot of time and discomfort to figure that out. The year I turned 30, I changed my legal name, found a nice plastic surgeon, and sent my tits away to live in a nice farm upstate. The year after that, I started using singular *they* pronouns. I tried several variations on "gender-neutral" clothing options before finally settling into a colorful femme wardrobe, because that feels like home to me. I'm not sure what comes next. By the time this book comes out, I might be on HRT, or recovering from a hysterectomy, or I might have changed nothing at all and settled into this version of my body as home.

There are infinite possible ways to be trans, and none of us will have identical journeys. *You* are the only expert on your own way, and you get to decide for yourself what works for you and what doesn't. As I write this book, *I am deferring to your expertise in the vital subject of your own gender.* I trust you to know what feels right for you. Take what works for you and ignore the rest.

My hope is that this book will give you comfort, a few new coping mechanisms, and most importantly, a firm sense that you are not alone in this gender thing.

You and I, we're not alone.

And we're *marvelous*.

CHAPTER 1
WHO I AM

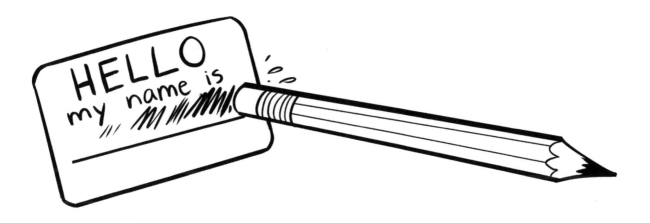

How Do You Identify?

That's a really big and complicated question for many of us. It's okay if your identity doesn't fit on a neat little line, or if you're not sure how to answer. A better question might be: How would you describe your gender? What words and identity labels have you used for it in the past? What words would you like to use?

Most trans people I've spoken to about their gender identities have at some point been hesitant to use the word *trans* to describe themselves. It's a small word with a big weight. I've heard all the reasons: calling themselves trans felt too vulnerable, they weren't ready to address it, they didn't think they could use the word if they hadn't transitioned yet, they weren't trans enough to call themselves trans. That last one comes up a lot: "I didn't think I was trans enough."

Trans identity is a broad umbrella. There's room enough for you. If you're reading this book to examine your own gender identity, you're trans enough. You are allowed to call yourself trans, even if it's just between the pages of this book. If later you realize it doesn't fit you, that's okay! Identity changes and evolves. But right now, if you want it, the word *trans* is yours.

Certificate of Transness

This certificate verifies that

_____ *(name)*

is trans enough to identify as

_____ *(identity/label)*

and anyone who says otherwise can go eat rocks

And, And, And...

People might treat you like you can only have a single identity, like being trans AND disabled, or trans AND Black, or trans AND a lesbian is too much. Those same people are invariably ignoring their own intersections of identity, usually because their identities fit what society treats as "normal"—straight, cisgender, white, able-bodied, neurotypical, etc. They aren't any more or less normal than you or I, and you aren't "too much" for having intersecting identities that are different from theirs.

Where do your identities intersect?

I am _____ and _____ and _____ .

I am _____ and _____ and _____ .

I am _____ and _____ and _____ .

Where do these intersections give you a unique perspective? How do your intersecting identities add to who you are?

_____

_____

_____

_____

_____

_____

_____

_____

_____

It's okay to not know everything about my gender identity.

Affirmations: Does this Thing Actually Work?

In this book, we'll be doing a lot of positive affirmation exercises. They might sound cheesy, but positive affirmations can help you reshape the way you think about yourself and respond to stress. Get ready for some science!

A 2011 study by psychology researchers at multiple universities and the National Cancer Institute found significant evidence that self-affirmations improve problem solving under stress:

Self-affirmation may be considered as one process that operates as part of a psychological immune system that is engaged when individuals experience self-threats... Just as the body's immune system responds to pathogens and protects against disease by identifying and killing foreign invaders and tumor cells, the psychological immune system initiates protective adaptations under impending threats to the self.[1]

Basically, just like getting enough sleep and taking your vitamins can help your body's resilience against illness, self-affirmation can help your mind's resilience against negative experiences.

A 2009 study published in *Health Psychology*[2] also found that having undergraduate students do self-affirmations about their core values before stressful midterm exams reduced the stress hormones in their bodies during their exams. Affirming other parts of your self outside of the part that feels threatened can help you cope with the threatened part, too. Because of that, some of the self-affirmations in this book will seem like they have nothing to do with gender. I promise they're valuable, too.

Some studies have even found that practicing self-affirmation affects physical health, because stress is linked with a lower immune response and self-affirmation helps lessen the body's stress response.

---

1   David K. Sherman and Kimberly A. Hartson (2011) 'Reconciling Self-Protection with Self-Improvement: Self-Affirmation Theory.' In Mark D. Alicke and Constantine Sedikides (eds) *Handbook of Self-Enhancement and Self-Protection* (Chapter 6). New York: Guilford Press.

2   David K. Sherman, D.P. Bunyan, J.D. Creswell, J.D. and L.M. Jaremka (2009) 'Psychological vulnerability and stress: The effects of self-affirmation on sympathetic nervous system responses to naturalistic stressors.' *Health Psychology* 28, 5, 554–562. Available at: https://doi.org/10.1037/a0014663

Across the board, studies on this subject have found that self-affirmations have the biggest impact on people with the highest stress, including people making high-stakes decisions, people with higher stress reactions, and minorities working against an unfairly stacked system.

So let's practice some self-affirmations, and the next time someone with a fifth grade understanding of biology tries to fake-science your identity out of existence, you can science your brain out of letting them bother you.

Gender Identity Affirmations

Repeat the affirmations below. If writing longhand doesn't work for you, try saying them to yourself in the mirror or turning the ones you need most into a chant.

My gender identity is an important part of who I am.

My identity deserves respect.

There is no wrong way to be trans.

I am the expert on my own gender.

I am allowed to change my mind, my pronouns, and the labels I use for myself.

My gender identity is mine.

No one can tell me who to be.

I am the best authority on who I am.

I trust myself to do what's best for me.

I love myself, and I love who I'm becoming.

What do you need to hear about your gender identity? Write your own affirmations below. If you have recurring negative thoughts about your gender identity ("My gender identity isn't as legitimate as other people's"), try turning its opposite into an affirmation ("My gender identity is just as valid as other people's"). Keep your language positive and sincere.

Journal prompt: Write about three times you've felt truly like *yourself*.

What do those three times have in common?

What little things about them can you repeat for yourself to capture that feeling again?

_____

_____

_____

_____

_____

_____

_____

_____

_____

Little Things that Go a Long Way

Little things can make a big impact about how you feel about yourself. Here are some suggestions from other trans folks:

- Identify clothing items that make you feel good and put them right up front in your closet so you'll reach for them more

- Wear nail polish or makeup that makes you feel powerful. If you're new to makeup, look up tutorials online and try new things

- Take off makeup, clothes, or other gendered trappings you're not feeling good about

- Ask a trusted friend to call you by a new name for a day to try it out

- Shave your facial hair. Treat the skin underneath to a facial

- Pay special care to your facial hair

- Try something new with your hair

- Practice a new walk: If you walk from the knees, engage your hips more, or vice versa. Try a dainty walk, a walk with swagger, a precise walk

- Play with your voice. Do you speak from your chest or your head? (People raised male tend to use their chest voice, while people raised female tend to use their head voice.) Try speaking from the one you don't tend to use

- What makes you feel good exploring your gender? What do you want to try?

- _____

- _____

- _____

- _____

- _____

Drawing exercise: How do you want the world to see you?

I am the only one who gets to define me.

Burn the Thoughts that Hold You Back

Write down the thoughts that stop you from pursuing your gender identity.

_____

_____

_____

_____

_____

_____

_____

_____

_____

_____

_____

_____

Now destroy them. If you have safe access to a fire, tear out this page and burn it. If you don't have safe access to a fire, take a marker, paint, or decorative tape and cover those words. (If you have strong feelings about tearing up books, you can also do this exercise on a piece of scrap paper.)

Naming Yourself

Are you looking for a new name that fits you? Let's brainstorm!

What characteristics do you want for your name? (Classic or unusual, certain sounds or syllables, meanings you'd like to convey, etc.)

_____

_____

_____

_____

Names you love on other people or characters:

_____

_____

_____

_____

Names or nicknames you've used that felt good:

_____

_____

_____

_____

Find some new ones! Look on baby name websites and ask trusted friends.
What new names do you like?

_____

_____

_____

_____

Circle the ones you like most from all these lists. Try signing your full name
and see how it feels. Does anything stand out as more "you"?

_____

_____

_____

_____

Write after me: *I am trans enough.*
Keep writing that sentence. Fill this page with it.

CHAPTER 2
SELF-WORTH

In her TED Talk "The Power of Vulnerability," shame researcher Brené Brown says that we should raise children to know that they don't need to be perfect to be worthy. She says we all need to hear "You're imperfect, and you're wired for struggle, but you are worthy of love and belonging."[3]

Has anyone told you that before? Can you accept the idea that you are enough exactly as you are, flaws included?

This is what self-worth is about. You don't need to think you're perfect, because no one is. Self-worth is knowing that you deserve love and belonging regardless of your imperfections.

You do. I promise.

---

3   TED (2011, January 3) *The Power of Vulnerability/Brené Brown/TED Talks* [Video file]. Retrieved from https://www.youtube.com/watch?v=iCvmsMzlF7o&feature=emb_title

My Core Values

What are your core values—the values that make you *you*? What matters to you most in life?

_____

_____

_____

_____

_____

_____

_____

_____

Self-Worth Affirmations

Repeat the affirmations below. If writing longhand doesn't work for you, try saying them to yourself in the mirror or turning the ones you need most into a chant.

I am worthy.

_____

I am good enough.

_____

I am smart and capable.

_____

I trust myself.

_____

I do good for the people I care about.

_____

I take care of the people I care about.

_____

I deserve to feel good about my identity.

_____

I deserve to transition in the way I feel is best for me.

_____

My gender identity is not an inconvenience.

_____

I do not need to adapt to other people's expectations.

_____

I deserve kindness.

_____

I deserve respect.

_____

I deserve to be loved.

_____

I deserve to be taken care of.

_____

I love myself exactly as I am.

_____

What do you need to hear about your own worth? Write your own affirmations below. If you have recurring negative thoughts about your self-worth ("I am such a jerk"), try turning its opposite into an affirmation ("I am doing my best to be kind"). Keep your language positive and sincere.

_____

_____

_____

_____

_____

_____

_____

Journal prompt: What would your life be like if you believed everything you just wrote?

My gender identity is one of the many lovable things about me.

Journal prompt: Write about someone you know who deserves everything good that happens to them. What do you admire about them? What traits do you share with them?

Caring for Myself

What can you do to be kind to yourself? Consider these questions, and then fill this page with ideas for things you can do to care for yourself:

What helps you relax? What songs, movies, or other media make you feel happy, energized, or content? How do you treat yourself on sick days? What makes you feel comfortable in your space?

Look back to the "Little Things that Go a Long Way" exercise in Chapter 1 for more ideas.

It's okay to not love every aspect of my gender.

Guilt and Shame

Guilt and shame are weights that we all carry at some point in our lives, and they have an incredible impact on the way we see ourselves. If you want to work on your self-worth, one of the most valuable things you can learn is how to tell the difference between guilt and shame.

In their simplest forms, guilt tells you "I did something bad," while shame tells you "I *am* something bad."

Guilt is a useful emotion that pushes you toward positive action, like apologizing to someone you've hurt, fixing a mess you contributed to, or helping others. Guilt lessens when you take action.

Shame is not a useful emotion. To quote shame and vulnerability researcher Brené Brown: "Shame is the most powerful, master emotion. It's the fear that we're not good enough." Shame pushes you toward self-destructive action and has been linked to addiction, depression, aggression, eating disorders, and suicide. Shame doesn't offer a useful solution, and it doesn't lessen with action: It festers. It breeds more fear, which breeds more shame.

Let's practice distinguishing between guilt and shame. Fill in the table below to help sort out your own feelings.

Topic	How it makes me feel	What it wants me to do	Guilt or shame?
Taking my cat to the emergency vet	Sick to my stomach	Pay more attention to my cat's health	Guilt
Taking my cat to the emergency vet	Like I don't deserve to have pets	Feel like a terrible pet owner	Shame

Topic	How it makes me feel	What it wants me to do	Guilt or shame?

As Brené Brown emphasizes in her work, shame thrives when it's allowed to fester in secret, but it cannot survive being shared. When you're ready to let go of a shame on this list from the table above, talk to someone who you trust to respond with empathy.

I deserve to feel happy, safe, and loved.

Validation

Everyone needs validation. When you're living in a social climate where your gender identity is treated as a joke, a threat to others, or something you made up to feel special, validation is especially valuable.

What makes you feel more comfortable or certain about who you are? If you don't have an answer off the top of your head, look at what makes you feel invalidated or shaky in your identity—how can you do the opposite of that?

It's okay to ask for validation from people who care about you! Think about the people in your life you would trust to do that. It can be anyone, in person or online, and as simple as saying, "I'm feeling kind of low. Could you reassure me that [insert whatever makes you feel validated]?"

If you like non-verbal reassurance, you can always ask social media for gifts of cat pictures. The internet will always provide cat pictures. (If you prefer pictures of something else, the internet will usually provide that, too.)

Living with Fear

"Fear loves you more than anyone. But like anyone who loves you, fear can give bad advice."

Teri Blauersouth, mental health therapist

Like most of our uncomfortable emotions, fear serves an important purpose: It's a survival tool. All your fear wants is to keep you safe. Having a healthy relationship with your fear means being able to assess risks in a helpful way and acknowledge your fears without being overwhelmed by them.

Like any minority identity, being trans comes with certain risks that the majority population doesn't have to face, like receiving rejection, public harassment, or violence based on your gender identity. I'm not going to sugar coat it: Those are legitimate concerns. But knowing those risks does not mean your fear needs to dictate your life. It's important to cohabitate with uncomfortable feelings, even when they are loud, messy roommates.

Write a letter to your fear. What is it doing right? How is it hindering you? What can you learn from it? How can you use it to motivate you?

_____

_____

_____

_____

_____

_____

_____

_____

Do you have any other lingering uncomfortable emotions you'd like to address? Anger and jealousy are common feelings that come up with transition. This space is all yours—pick an emotion and write it a letter (or a poem, or a drunk text) here.

_____

_____

_____

_____

_____

_____

_____

_____

Write about a time you felt really good about who you are. What caused that feeling? What did it feel like in your mind and/or body? What can you do to repeat that feeling, even just a little bit?

I am enough, even when I feel incomplete.

Draw a world where trans rights are universal.

I won't wait until after I transition to follow my dreams.

CHAPTER 3
BODY IMAGE

Body image is a touchy subject for most people, but being trans adds a unique layer of difficulty. It can be a challenge accepting your body when you're facing dysphoria, clothes and social expectations that were made for a different body type, and a loud cultural narrative says you're "trapped in the wrong body."

For some of us, the idea that we're trapped in the wrong body can be helpful. For others, it can be toxic, putting us even more at odds with bodies that need and deserve special attention.

Personally, I prefer thinking of my body the way poet and activist Ollie Schminkey[4] does in their poem "Boobs," that regardless of other complicated feelings, "I am not trapped in my body. I am trapped in other people's perceptions of my body... I was not born into the wrong body. I was born into a world that does not know what my body means."

Maybe you're already at peace with your body. Maybe it's all a tangle of

---

4   Ollie's spoken word poem is available on YouTube at: www.youtube.com/watch?v=Pi7Vss4GYks

tense emotions. Wherever you're at, it's okay to feel the way you feel about your body. And however you feel about your body, your body—and you with it—deserves to be cared for.

Body Image Affirmations

Repeat the affirmations below. If writing longhand doesn't work for you, try saying them to yourself in the mirror or turning the ones you need most into a chant.

My body is part of who I am.

My body deserves kindness.

My body deserves nourishment and rest.

My body is valuable.

My body is unique.

My body doesn't need to look like anyone else's.

My worth is not dependent on my body.

My body is doing its best.

This body is mine, and I will shape it however I like.

I am beautiful.

I forgive my body for not always being what I need.

What do you need to hear about your body? Write your own affirmations below. If you have recurring negative thoughts about your body ("My body is gross"), try turning its opposite into an affirmation ("My body is lovely"). Keep your language positive and sincere.

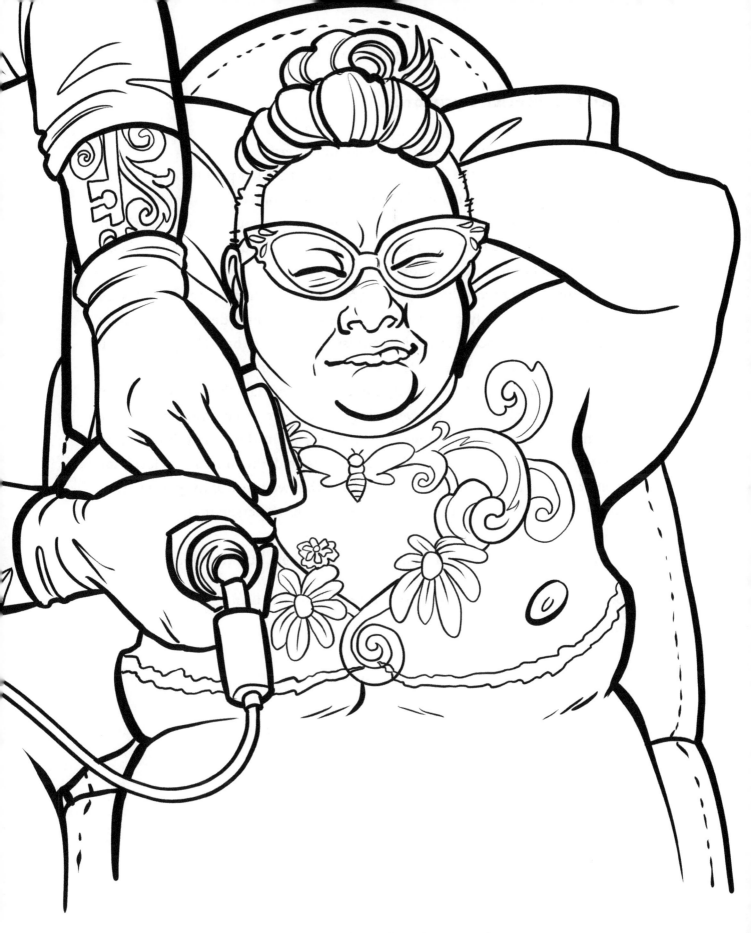

My body is mine and I will make it my home.

Social vs Internal Dysphoria

Dysphoria falls into two categories: social and internal.

Social dysphoria is the dysphoria you feel about other people's expectations of you. For example, the discomfort you feel when someone misgenders you in public is social dysphoria. You might alter your appearance or even transition medically or surgically to avoid it, but at the end of the day, this dysphoria is about societal gender expectations, not about you.

Internal dysphoria is the dysphoria you feel even when you're alone. I think of it as "desert island dysphoria." If you were stranded on a desert island all by yourself, with no concern about being misgendered, are there things you would still feel dysphoric about? If so, that's internal dysphoria.

Social dysphoria and internal dysphoria often overlap. For one person, top surgery feels vital to their own wellbeing on a core, internal level. For another person, they might not have any strong feelings about their chest, but they seek top surgery because it will help them avoid misgendering on a social level, for safety or comfort or both. For a third person, the two types of dysphoria are a tangle right in the center of their chest. And a fourth person might not even feel dysphoria! (More on that later.)

Where do your dysphoria feelings fit? Write them into the table below.

Social dysphoria	Internal dysphoria	Both

Draw your dysphoria. How do you experience dysphoria?
In the picture below, draw your dysphoria where you feel it.
There are no rules for how you express this.

Draw your dysphoria like it was a living creature.

Let's write a little story about your dysphoria creature.

I was on my way to _____ [place] when _____
[dysphoria name] jumped out of a bush, brandishing a _____
[noun] and a frown. "Time to feel _____ [negative adjective]
about yourself!" it cried, hitting me in the ankle.

I _____ [verb-ed] past it, hailing a taxi cab. The taxi smelled
like _____ [noun], but the driver seemed nice. Before we
could get to my destination, the car's brakes squealed and there was a loud
_____ [noise]. Good thing I was wearing my seatbelt, because
_____ [dysphoria name] had jumped onto the windshield!

"Listen to me, _____ [insulting name]!" it hollered. "I'm an expert
in _____ [subject you don't like]!"

This _____ [unpleasant adjective] thing wasn't going to give up.

"Just take me back home," I told the driver. _____ [dysphoria
name] slid off the windshield as the car turned around.

When we got to my house, I tipped the driver _____ [amount of
money] for the trouble.

A familiar voice cackled behind me, and I turned to find a flaming bag of
_____ [noun] on my doorstep.

Dammit, _____ [dysphoria name]. Not again.

You Do Not Need to Have Physical Dysphoria to Be Trans

Yeah, you read that right. We tend to think that dysphoria is a given for trans people, both because dysphoria is incredibly common and because dysphoria is used as a tool for healthcare providers to decide who gets transition-related treatment.

Gender identity is about how you see yourself on the inside. For many of us, how we see ourselves on the inside conflicts with our outsides in a way that causes discomfort. Some of us are able to make peace with that internal conflict or don't feel it as acutely, and that's okay.

We have spent decades fighting for acceptance based on the cis-centric world's idea that trans identity is defined by dysphoria. It's easy to internalize that idea when it seems like the whole world is pushing it at you.

It's okay to be in pain because of your gender. That pain doesn't define your identity.

It's okay to not be in pain because of your gender. It doesn't make you any less trans.

I do not need to meet a minimum level of misery to call myself trans.

Transition Is Not a One Size Fits All

Your body does not have to look a certain way to be trans. You do not need to transition in certain obligatory ways to be trans. Frankly, you don't need to change a damn thing if you don't want to.

We all know the typical medical transition narrative: Take X medication, do Y and Z surgeries, and ta-dah! You're done.

That narrative doesn't work for all of us, and even those of us who follow it to the letter don't end up looking or presenting the same. Every trans woman is not a perfectly polished femme goddess. Every trans man is not a bearded, plaid-clad beefcake. Every non-binary person is not a skinny, white, androgynous person. Those people do exist and are fabulous, but they're not representative of all of us.

Medical transition isn't an option for every trans person. Many of us can't afford surgery, can't take hormones for medical reasons, or aren't able to access transition-related medical services. Also, making permanent changes to your body is a big deal, and it's totally reasonable to just not want to have surgery or take medication. You're still trans if you don't medically transition.

Social transition isn't an option for every trans person. Some of us have allergies to makeup products, bodies that don't fit into another gender's typical clothes, budgets that don't allow for new clothes or a haircut. Some of us are living in hostile communities or are financially dependent on people who aren't safe to come out to.

Some of us will never "pass" as our correct gender because of the way our bodies are built. Some of us don't even want to pass, and that's okay.

You do not need to fit anyone else's idea of what a trans person looks like.

Do what feels right for you.

*My gender presentation is for me,
and it can be whatever I want it to be.*

Exercises for Body Positivity and Neutrality

Think about a part of your body you genuinely like. It can be something big, like your arms, something small, like your left eyebrow, or something more abstract, like your body's resilience. Name the thing you like about your body. Write about why you like this part of your body. What has it done for you? How do you feel when you think about it?

Now think about a part of your body you have no particular feelings about. Try to give it the same treatment as the part you wrote about before. Name the body part you feel neutral about. Write three positive things about it.

_____

_____

_____

_____

The next time you're feeling overwhelmed by negative feelings about your body, take a deep breath and focus on one of these body parts. Imagine that body part glowing with a calm, soft light. When you breathe in, picture that calm light spreading out through the rest of your body slowly. Breathe the light into your body for a count of 10, and then release it. This visualization exercise is also useful for general anxiety.

Coping with Body Changes

Even aside from transition, your body is a constantly shifting landscape. Being human means occasionally looking down at yourself and going "Whoa, that wasn't there before!"

Here are a few body changes that could happen to you, depending on your age and your plumbing:

- Puberty
- Second puberty (this one hits in your twenties and is less profound than the first)
- HRT-induced puberty
- Major injuries
- Pregnancy
- Menopause
- Hair loss

- Loss of strength
- Loss of mobility
- Degenerative conditions
- Medication side effects
- Weight loss or gain
- Serious illness
- Surgical alterations

Which of these have happened to you? Which were voluntary and which weren't? What did you learn from them about coping with major body changes?

_____

_____

_____

_____

_____

_____

_____

Connecting with Your Body

For many of us, our bodies feel more like a source of conflict or a foreign object than a part of us. You don't have to love your body, but it is yours, and you deserve to live in it fully. What makes you feel connected to your body in a positive or neutral way? Let's brainstorm. Here are some ideas to think about:

What activities engage your senses? What makes you feel strong, flexible, or physically capable? What makes you feel attractive? What makes your body feel good?

My identity is not defined by pain.

CHAPTER 4
COMING OUT

Coming out of the closet is not a one-time event. It's a rolling process of deciding who you want to know about your identity. Coming out takes courage. It's an act of vulnerability and trust, and you are brave as hell for doing it. You also don't owe your truth to anyone you don't trust with it. Remember these things.

The easiest coming out I ever had was early on, with my lesbian roommate. I was headed out to dinner with friends, and on my way out the door, I blurted out, "By the way, I'm genderqueer, and I want to start going by Theo."

My roommate glanced up from her book, smiled, and said, "Okay, Theo. Any pronoun change?"

"Not at the moment," I said.

"Cool," she said. "Let me know if that changes." She went back to her book.

It was so easy, such a relief, that I felt like I was floating three inches off the ground for the rest of the night.

This has been my internal template for the ideal coming out experience ever since. It made me feel welcome, loved, and normal.

What is your ideal coming out experience? What does the other person say to you? How does it make you feel? You can draw from experience or make up your own.

How Others React

Figuring out whether someone will support you when you come out isn't a simple yes/no. Sometimes people who are otherwise unsupportive of the LGBTQ+ community will start to come around when they find out that someone they love is a member of that community. Sometimes people who are supportive of us in theory have a harder time accepting us when faced with the reality that someone they love is LGBTQ+. Factors like religion, personal background, politics, and what media a person consumes can all sway a person's reaction.

People who mean well can react poorly at first. Give them time, share resources with them, and let them talk it out with people they trust who *aren't you*.

People who haven't been supportive in the past might also surprise you with acceptance.

You can't predict or control how someone else reacts, but you can control how YOU react. You can choose to give them the chance to accept or reject you, instead of pre-rejecting yourself on their behalf.

The Stages of Change

I'm the sort of person who sits with decisions for a long time. For example, it took me three months to pick my current electric teakettle. It's a $20 kettle. There weren't major life stakes to picking the "wrong" electric kettle, and yet I pored over every cheap electric kettle listing on the internet, feeling like Indiana Jones deciding between beverage containers in the chamber of the Holy Grail.

Change can be hard, is what I'm saying—even when you want it.

By the time of the Kettle Inquisition, I was used to admonishing myself for my indecision. I beat myself up for not coming out as bi in college, "wasting" my prime girl-kissing years. I beat myself up for being slow to admit my gender identity to myself. And the crowning jewel of my regret, the display of indecision that is still difficult for me to think about: I didn't come out to my uncle before he died.

I knew I was trans. I knew my small town uncle probably wouldn't get it, but he'd love me anyway. He had pancreatic cancer. In the two years I spent trying to work up the nerve to tell him who I was, he was declared terminal, and on a sunny August day in 2013, I got the call letting me know he'd died.

Regret is hard. I can't give you a coloring page that will fix it. What I can do is help you understand the way your brain manages decision-making, which might make the process of coming out (or buying a new kettle) a little easier.

The Stages of Change is a psychological model developed by James O. Prochaska and Carlo DiClemente in the late 1970s. Originally used to help patients make positive health changes like quitting smoking, it applies to so many areas of life that it's become pretty much ubiquitous in psychology.

This is the process your brain goes through when you try to make decisions, especially major ones that will affect your life going forward. It's not as simple as "just do it!"

STAGES of CHANGE

CONTEMPLATION
considering change

DECISION
deciding to change

PRE-CONTEMPLATION
not considering change

ACTIVE CHANGE
actually making the change

RELAPSE
returning to pre-change

MAINTENANCE
following through on the change

Pre-contemplation: I *won't* do the thing.

At this point, no amount of nudging or advice from well-meaning friends will make you want to move forward. Denial might be involved.

Example: You don't need to come out to that person, it's fine, you're fine.

Contemplation: Okay, but *what if* I did the thing?

You might need to learn more about the thing or talk your feelings about the thing out with someone. Advice and nudging are still not helpful at this point and might make you feel unfairly pressured.

Example: The idea of coming out to that person has crossed your mind. It might be nice to have them know who you really are, but it's also scary, and you're not sure you want to risk telling them. You weigh the pros and cons. You're not ready to decide yet. When a friend gives you advice on the subject, you don't want to listen to them.

Decision: I *will do* the thing.

You've decided, you're making a plan, and you're open to advice. This is the point where you ask for help if you need it.

Example: You're pretty sure you're going to come out to that person. You're figuring out how best to do it, and maybe you're talking it out with your therapist or a trusted friend. When a friend gives you advice on the subject, you actually consider it.

Active change: I am *doing* the thing!

You're doing it! You're making the change!

Example: You come out to that person. It's nerve-wracking, but it's done. You might have new decisions to make now.

Maintenance stage: Standing by your decision.

You've executed your decision, and now it's time to stick to your guns. This might be very easy or it might be surprisingly difficult, depending on the decision you made and how big a change it is. Loved ones can help you stick to your decision.

Example: When the person you just came out to uses your dead name, you gently correct them. When it happens in a group setting, your friend might correct that person for you or reinforce your decision by using your correct name and pronouns in front of the person you just came out to. You might reinforce your coming out by signaling it, like wearing a pronoun pin, changing your name and pronouns on your social media bio, or requesting a new name tag at work.

After the change is made, you might fully adopt the change or relapse into pre-change ways. In our coming out example, adopting the change means you continue to live out and proud to the person or people you've come out to; relapsing would mean going back into the closet, allowing that person to use your old name and pronouns because it's convenient for them.

Let's write about a time when you made an important decision about your gender identity. What did the stages of change look like for you? Are there any stages you felt like you spent longer in than others? What did you need from others in each stage?

Coming Out Affirmations

Repeat the affirmations below. If writing longhand doesn't work for you, try saying them to yourself in the mirror or turning the ones you need most into a chant.

My identity is important.

Who I am is not up for debate.

My gender is real and valid.

I am the only one who gets to define my identity.

It is not my job to comfort people who don't like who I am.

I will give others the chance to listen to me.

I am brave.

I am resilient.

My voice is important.

_____

I will come out at the right time.

_____

I trust my instincts about who is safe.

_____

I deserve support.

_____

I deserve to be loved unconditionally.

_____

I am lovable and important.

_____

What do you need to hear about coming out? Write your own affirmations below. If you have recurring negative thoughts about coming out ("I'm going to be rejected by everyone"), try turning its opposite into an affirmation ("I deserve to be accepted"). Keep your language positive and sincere.

_____

_____

_____

_____

Should I come out to this person?
This flowchart is just one way to decide whether to come out. Where does it differ from your own decision-making process?

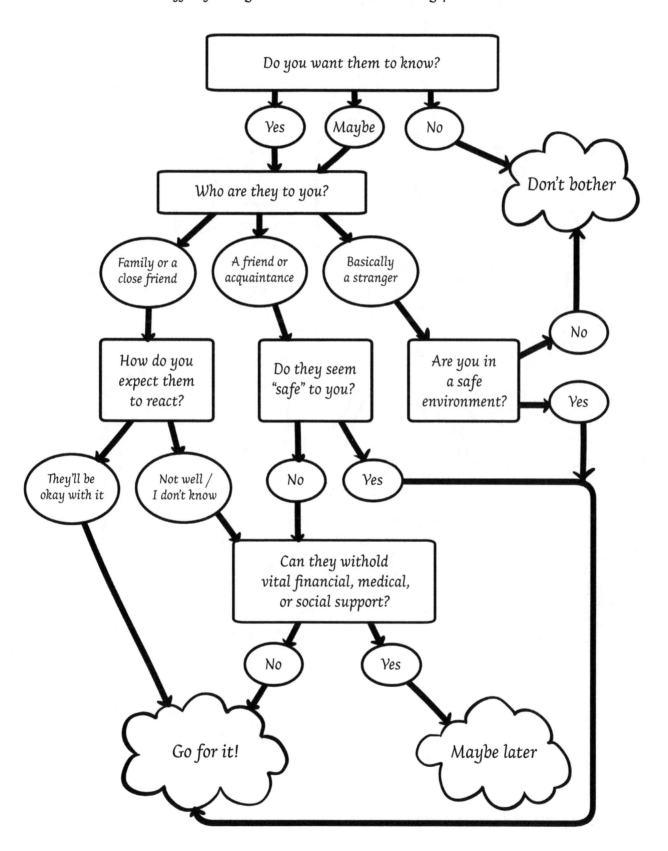

Being out and proud doesn't mean I have to out myself to everyone I meet.

Coming Out Plan

Who do you want to come out to?

_____

What do you want to say to them?

_____

_____

_____

_____

Reread what you just wrote. Is there anything in it that needs to be defined or revised to help this person understand it?

_____

_____

_____

_____

What is their current level of understanding on the subject of gender? If they need education, what websites or books could you recommend to them?

_____

_____

_____

_____

How would you like to tell this person—in person, in a letter, over email? In what scenarios are they most receptive to change?

_____

_____

_____

_____

_____

_____

_____

_____

Let's brainstorm some kind things that would make you feel good after coming out. Flip back to the "Caring for Myself" exercise in Chapter 2 to find ideas for things that make you feel good about yourself. Which of these could you do for yourself? Do you need to prepare anything?

_____

_____

_____

_____

_____

_____

For more resources on this topic, check out The Trevor Project's "Coming Out As You," a collection of resources to prepare you to come out, including readings, worksheets, and handy suggestions.[5]

---

5   See www.thetrevorproject.org/about/programs-services/coming-out-as-you

Post-Coming Out Exercise

Who did you come out to?

What did you say to them?

How did they react?

How did that make you feel?

What coping skills did you use to deal with their reaction?

_____

_____

_____

_____

What did you do for yourself afterwards?

_____

_____

_____

_____

What do you need right now? How can you be kind to yourself in this moment?

_____

_____

_____

_____

An FAQ for Clueless Loved Ones (and Less-Than-Loved Ones)

Here is a list of some common less-than-helpful statements and sample scripts for how to respond to them.[6]

Why do we have so many labels? We don't need all these labels

"We have all these labels because gender can be many different things. Labels help us find each other and communicate who we are to the world."

Does this mean you're gay?

"Gender and sexuality are two different things. Gender identity is about who you want to be, and sexuality is about who you want to be with."

Optional follow-up: "But yes, Grandma, I'm gay."

You're too young to know what you are

"When you were my age, did you know you were [their gender]?"

This is coming out of nowhere!

"I understand how it might seem sudden to you, but I've been figuring out my identity privately for a long time."

This transgender thing is just a trend!

"Archaeologists have found art, remains, and records of trans people dating back over 4500 years across multiple continents, and in the past few decades we've finally been recognized by mainstream society because of medical and social advances."

Alternately: "We're talking about people, not slap bracelets."

You just want attention

"If all I wanted was attention, I'd do something way cheaper and less emotionally difficult with WAY more glitter involved."

When are you getting The Surgery?, or Have you had The Surgery?

"My private medical plans are between me and my doctor."

Or "That question hits a little below the belt...literally."

Or ask them about their next visit with their gynecologist or urologist and see how comfortable they are talking about their genital health with you. (Note: This is to create maximum awkwardness, and when employed on over-sharers it may backfire.)

Well, I identify as an attack helicopter

This meme from 2014 is tired, insulting, and *everywhere*, especially online.

Give them the pamphlet on the next page. Be aggressively supportive of their attack helicopter transition until they admit they're so sick of it that they'll never make this tired joke again.

---

6   You can also refer them to online resources like www.glaad.org/transgender/transfaq

So you want to be an Attack Helicopter

An introduction to your new identity

Resources:

Just stop it.

Best of luck with your identity!

You're going to need it.

Congratulations on coming to terms with your identity!

You are on the forefront of an exciting new category of identity! While LGBTQIA+ identities are based on scientifically proven biological and psychological realities, your identity as an attack helicopter is completely based on self-identifying.

You're in the vanguard!

Unlike transitioning between genders, becoming an attack helicopter is physically impossible. You might have to wait for several decades before the technology exists to install rotary blades on your head.

In the meantime, instead of taking out your frustration on trans people, you should find a new hobby. Here are a few suggestions:

Knitting or crochet
Jogging
Pottery
Tabletop gaming
Archery
Painting miniatures
Baking
Yoga
Scrabble
Reading a book
Hiking
Volunteering
Minding your own business
Taxidermy

Unfortunately, there is no social movement dedicated to the rights of people who identify as attack helicopters.

This might be because people who identify as attack helicopters are not oppressed in any way whatsoever, as opposed to queer and trans people, who face discrimination in every realm of society, experience higher rates of abuse, murder, and suicide than other populations, and still have to fight for basic human rights even in most advanced nations in the world.

Or it could be because you're engaging in a boring, overused joke.

Coming Out Form

If you need to come out to someone you can't be bothered with, use the letter template below!

I am a(n) _____ [your gender identity here]. My name is
_____ and my pronouns are _____ .

I need you to stop _____ [negative behavior] because it makes
me feel _____ [emotion/swearing].

You can support me by _____ [action].

Have a(n) _____ [adjective] day.

Hi, I'm Trans

(Draw yourself or paste a photo here)

My name is _____
and my pronouns are _____

Cool

Alright

Awesome

I love that name!

Fantastic

Neato

Thanks for telling me

How wonderful

Nice

CHAPTER 5
MY COMMUNITY

Finding Safe People

What clues flag a person as "safe" to you? For example, when I first met one of my neighbors, I noticed that he had a pro-marriage equality sign hanging out on his porch from our state's 2013 vote. That he supported LGBTQ+ rights enough to donate to that initiative at a critical time made me feel instantly safer around him.

What little clues have you noticed in other people—their behavior, dress, homes, etc.—that make them feel safe to you?

Who do you know supports you? Think about who you could call in the middle of the night with a crisis. List three people, along with a way to contact them. This can include anyone: friends, family, teachers, colleagues, internet friends, religious leaders, doctors, therapists...

Tell these three people that they occupy this role in your life. People like to know that they're trusted. Offer to be the person they can call in the middle of the night, too.

Finding Trans Friends and Allies

Where can you find trans people and allies to befriend? We exist in every level of society, so somewhere there's a group of trans people or allies who share your interests. It might be harder if you live in a small town or somewhere especially inhospitable to LGBTQIA people, but I promise your community is out there.

Here are some ideas to start with:

👥 Look to the people you're already close to. Your community doesn't have to be new just because your pronouns are—it can be people you've known for years

👥 Examine the people on the periphery of your social network. Who would you like to know better? Who has common interests? Who seems trustworthy? Anyone you can name for all these three questions is a great candidate for friendship

👥 Ask trans and/or queer friends to introduce you to other friends who are safe

👥 If you're in school, look for school organizations that are for LGBTQIA[7] students or tend to collect LGBTQIA students. (The art and theater departments in my schools were always chock full o' gay folks, but your school might be different)

👥 Go to Pride events and take notes—or if Pride is long past, look up your nearest city's Pride website. What groups do you see with booths or floats at Pride that interest you? Attend their meetings or events

👥 Find online groups you might want to join by searching "[interest you have] + LGBT"

👥 Attend trans rights protests and talk to the people around you

---

7   Just because a space is queer does not mean it's free from discrimination. Many of us have been burned by transphobia, racism, misogyny, ableism, fatphobia, and other unacceptable nonsense in queer spaces whose members like to think they're accepting. If you've experienced this, your feelings about those spaces are legitimate, and I have a bonus activity for you: Grab a piece of scrap paper and write down what you'd like to say to the people who hurt you. Let that anger and grief out. When you're done, burn that page (safely, outdoors) or destroy it with markers, paint, or decorative tape. Then go back to the "Caring for Myself" section in Chapter 2 and do some extra self-care.

👥 Look for local organizations that engage in hobbies you like and gauge for yourself how trans-friendly they are. You might find a place for yourself among unexpected allies at the local reptile rescue group, or with the competitive Rubik's Cube crowd

👥 Look for people and groups who share hobbies that allow you to play with gender, like costuming or cosplay, role-playing games, queer comics, or writing

👥 Search trans groups and hashtags on social media. Talk to people in those spaces

👥 Follow trans writers, artists, and activists online. Even if you don't make new friends from people who also follow them, having trans voices on your feed can help you feel connected to the broader trans community

👥 Keep your mind open to old friends. Sometimes people who didn't react well to your coming out can come around in time and be great allies. Let them reach out to you

Where are some places you've met trans people and allies?

_____

_____

_____

_____

Using the list above and your own knowledge of where you live online and off, brainstorm some places you might want to look for your community.

_____

_____

_____

I am not alone.

Journal prompt: What do you need from a community?

What makes you feel connected to a community? How can you invite more of that into your life? How can you provide that for others?

Community Affirmations

Repeat the affirmations below. If writing longhand doesn't work for you, try saying them to yourself in the mirror or turning the ones you need most into a chant.

I get to choose my own community.

I trust my instincts about people.

I am worthy of having friends.

I deserve love and respect.

I deserve to be treated as an equal.

I love and respect my friends.

I am an important part of my community.

My community supports me.

My chosen family is just as important as my family of origin.

It's okay to walk away from people who aren't good for me.

What do you need to hear about community? Write your own affirmations below. If you have recurring negative thoughts about your community ("No one truly loves me"), try turning its opposite into an affirmation ("I am truly loved"). Keep your language positive and sincere.

Chosen Family

The term "chosen family" originated in the LGBTQIA community as a way of describing the tight bonds we formed with our queer friends when our families of origin wouldn't have us. Your chosen family is the friends you decide to support and love like family: the roommate who might as well be your sibling; the friend whose child calls you their aunt, uncle, or entle; the people outside your family of origin with whom you build the community and traditions that anchor you. According to *Psychology Today*, 40 percent of homeless teens identify as queer, and 64 percent of queer baby boomers report having built and relied on chosen family. Chosen family is a queer institution, and it's one we get to build for ourselves.

My chosen family consists of my spouse, a handful of friends who are like siblings to me (and their children, who are now my nieces, nephews, and niblings), my younger friend we took in when she was a homeless trans teen, and my spouse's chosen family that I've acquired through marriage. These are people who were there for me when I first came out, people whose couches I slept on during crises, people who encourage and challenge me and love me and would pick me up from the airport even though they're not obligated to by blood.

Who would you count among your chosen family? What do they mean to you?

What can you do to show them your appreciation and love?

Sometimes a family is two parents and their children. Sometimes a family is a ragtag group of queers who chose each other.

Boundaries Are a Gift

A boundary is, as researcher/storyteller Brené Brown defines it, "simply our lists of what's okay and what's not okay." Setting boundaries is an act of compassion for yourself and the other person. When you tell someone "Here is my boundary," that gives them a handy instruction on what not to do, helps to prevent conflict between you, and opens communication so they can do the same for you.

When someone else sets a boundary with you, it doesn't mean they hate you or they're pushing you away. Try to react as you would like others to react when you set a boundary: respectfully, and not taking it as a personal attack.

> When we combine the courage to make clear what works for us and what doesn't with the compassion to assume people are doing their best, our lives change. Yes, there will be people who violate our boundaries, and this will require that we continue to hold those people accountable. But when we're living in our integrity, we're strengthened by the self-respect that comes from the honoring of our boundaries, rather than being flattened by disappointment and resentment.[8]

If you find yourself resenting someone in your life, it usually means there's a boundary you need to set or enforce with them. That doesn't mean it's your fault they did something you resent, but it does give you a clue about how to fix the situation.

What are your basic boundaries with friends? With families? Can you think of a time when someone violated a boundary with you and you found a resolution that felt good?

8   Brené Brown (2015) *Rising Strong*. London: Vermilion (Penguin), p.147.

Let's practice setting some healthy boundaries. A healthy boundary establishes a need and, if relevant, tells the person what you will do to support yourself if they do not cooperate. Healthy boundaries do not involve threats, withholding of the other person's needs, or humiliation. For example, "If you continue to deadname me, I'm not going to talk to you on the phone anymore" is a healthy and reasonable boundary. What are some other situations where you might need to set a boundary? What could you say to the other person?

Identifying and Removing Abusive People

Trans people are statistically more likely to suffer abuse than the general cisgender population. It's important to recognize the signs of emotional abuse as well as physical. Here is a short list of common red flags for abuse:

- They tell you that you can't do anything right

- They humiliate you (insults, demeaning your accomplishments, telling your friends stories they know will upset you)

- They try to control you (isolating you, controlling your finances, treating you like a child)

- They try to prevent you from transitioning (denying you access to medical resources, forcing you to dress like your gender of origin, etc.)

- They treat you like you're always the one in the wrong (false accusations, playing the victim when you point out the harm they've caused, denying things you know are true)

- They trivialize your feelings

- In a romantic relationship, they manipulate or force you into physical intimacy

- Their unpredictable behavior makes you feel like you're walking on eggshells

- They threaten to hurt you, your pets, or your children, or destroy your things

- They physically harm you, your pets, or your children on purpose

Abuse can happen in any kind of relationship, including with relatives, friends, romantic partners, professional contacts, and doctors.

You don't deserve to be treated like that. If you think someone in your life is abusive, reach out to a trusted third party, like a therapist. If you don't have a therapist (and I highly recommend getting one!), a friend or relative who isn't close to the possible abuser can also help. Talk out your feelings. Search online for abuse resources. If you're able, it might be good to go "no contact" with the abusive person.

I cut my abusive mother out of my life when I was 31 years old, after more than a decade of second chances and attempts to change her. The last straw wasn't her hostile reaction to my gender identity, although that was a big part of why I needed to get away. It wasn't the years of manipulation, gaslighting, and humiliation. It was a small thing, an easy boundary that shouldn't have been crossed, that made me realize this person would never stop treating me as less than worthy of her respect. She would never be the person I needed her to be.

After talking it over with my therapist, my partner, my brother, and a few empathetic friends, I made a plan to go no contact with my abuser. I sent her a short, firm email telling her I would no longer be in contact with her, blocked her on all media, and left for a sci-fi convention in another city for the weekend in case she came to my house.

Cutting that person out of my life is one of the most difficult and beneficial things I've ever done for myself. My self-worth and ability to trust myself grew in leaps and bounds in the years after. Before I went no contact I had trouble speaking up when I needed to, but now more often than not it's hard to make me shut up. I'm a happier, healthier person without her in my life.

Cutting contact isn't the right solution for everyone. When the person who isn't supporting you has a chance of coming around, you might want to give them that chance. When you're relying on them for financial, housing, or medical support, getting away from them might not be an option.

But if you can, and if you need to, it's okay to cut that person out of your life. Removing an abuser from your life doesn't make you a bad person. Be kind to yourself the way you wanted that person to be kind to you.

Asking for Help

Asking for help is one of the most vital and difficult aspects of being part of a community. A lot of us have trouble with asking for help—often because we've been burned before, but also because *vulnerability is hard.*

Vulnerability means exposing yourself—your true self—to others. Being vulnerable with someone might feel like being weak, but it takes a lot of courage. Coming out is vulnerable. Setting a boundary is vulnerable. Asking for help is especially vulnerable, but when you learn to do it, you'll be so much better off.

Why asking for help is good:

☕ It connects you with others. Vulnerability is the path to human connection. Communities thrive on cooperation

☕ People like to help each other! The person helping you gets an emotional boost from helping

☕ It puts you in a better position to empathize the next time someone else needs help

☕ It prevents you from suffering in silence, which is important because you don't deserve that

☕ How good are you at asking for help? Be honest

☕ _____

Are there any areas of your life where you could stand to ask for more help?

_____

_____

_____

_____

_____

_____

_____

_____

If someone treats you like a burden for asking for help, that's on them, not on you. It could be they haven't set a boundary with you that they need to do. It could be they're having a bad day unrelated to this. It's okay.

Sometimes people are even proud of you for asking for help. *I'm* proud of you for asking for help!

Write about a time when someone supported you in a way that felt right. What did they do? What about it worked for you? Have you told them how much it helped? How could you ask for that kind of support from others in the future?

_____

_____

_____

_____

_____

_____

_____

_____

Make a Misgender Jar

You will need

Paper

Tape

Scissors

An empty jar
with a lid

Writing implements

(Optional) stickers,
glitter, rhinestones

This is a great project for that social group that supports you but can't seem to remember your new name or pronouns. Decorate an empty jar with your name or pronouns. Anyone who misgenders you has to put a small fine into the jar.

Enlist a supportive friend to enforce the misgender jar. This works best when the group has a good sense of humour.

A misgender jar makes a great present for a trans friend who's just come out!

CHAPTER 6
BEING OUT IN THE WORLD

A Note on Safety

I want to tell you that the world is safe for us. I want to say, "Just get out there and be yourself," but we both know it's not that easy. Depending on where you live, your race, your social situation, and your ability to "pass" as your gender, being out and trans in the world can range from tricky to downright dangerous.

I can't tell you the world is safe for us. But I will tell you that this is our world, too, and we deserve to live in it however we want. We have the right to carve out spaces for ourselves. And, after fighting so hard to find our identities, don't we owe it to ourselves to be true to who we are, whenever possible?

The world isn't always safe for us, and we should get out in it anyway, because it's ours.

I am allowed to take up space in the world.

What makes you feel safer in public? Here's a list of things that other trans people have found make them feel safer when they're out in the world. Add your own at the bottom!

✚ Bringing friends or family

✚ Going places that are familiar

✚ Dressing up

✚ Wearing pronoun pins and pride flags OR leaving pronoun pins and pride flags at home

✚ Going places that have gender-neutral restrooms

✚ Going places that have staff or patrons who flag as LGBTQIA

✚ Going places where the staff have pronouns on their name tags

✚ Wearing gender-neutral or oversized clothing

✚ Wearing clothes that make you look more intimidating

✚ A fresh haircut or shave

✚ A hat or wig

✚ Perfecting your makeup

✚ Going to LGBTQIA-friendly spaces

✚ Being familiar with the people running an event

✚ Talking to a loved one on the phone while walking places

✚ Taking self-defense classes

✚ Steel-toed boots or sharp heels

✚ Pepper spray and other self-defense tools

✚ Traveling by car instead of public transit

✚ _____

✚
✚
✚
✚
✚
✚
✚

Being Out in the World Affirmations

Repeat the affirmations below. If writing longhand doesn't work for you, try saying them to yourself in the mirror or turning the ones you need most into a chant.

I deserve to be a part of this world.

I will enjoy the world around me.

I am responsible.

I am safe.

I will find or create a safer space for myself.

I trust myself to know my own limits.

I will not interact with trolls.

I will not compare myself to other trans people on the internet.

It is not my sole responsibility to educate people about my gender.

I am a vital part of this world.

What do you need to hear about being out in the world? Write your own affirmations below. If you have recurring negative thoughts about living in the world ("I should just be a hermit forever and get eaten by my cats"), try turning its opposite into an affirmation ("I deserve to enjoy the outside world and *not* get eaten by my cats"). Keep your language positive and sincere.

Getting Out and About

For many of us, getting out of the house can be a challenge. Dysphoria knocks you for a loop, you're at an awkward mid-transition point where your body isn't doing what you want it to do, you're afraid of not "passing," you know that one neighbor is going to side-eye you, your neighborhood isn't safe for trans folks... there are so many reasons to stay home.

But you can't lock yourself in your home forever. I challenge you to go out and be a trans person in the world! Fill in the categories on the chart below, mix and match one thing from each column, and get yourself out there.

What to wear	Places to go	Things to do	People to go with

How to Get Out of a Conversation about Your Gender

You're out in the world, and someone has taken that as permission to corner you into a conversation about your gender identity. How do you get out of it?

If the person seems well-meaning...

If you know them well enough to know they'll react okay, be frank with them: "I'd rather talk about [mutual interest] right now." If you're not sure how they'll react, ask them unrelated questions about themself. If you just want to get the hell out and the person isn't taking hints, making up an excuse like "Sorry, my cat is calling me" is totally fine.

If the person wants WAY too much information about your personal transition...

Politely highlight how invasive their questioning is with a line like "Do you ask everyone you meet about their [genitals/breasts/hormone levels]?" or "Usually I don't have the 'What's in my pants?' conversation until the third date." You can also turn it around on them and ask them the very same questions they're asking you, like "What does it feel like to have been born with a penis?"

If the person is acting like a jerk...

When someone is being a jerk about your gender, treat them like a toddler who's trying to give you a half-chewed slice of orange: Let them know you don't want it and give it back to them. Reflect their wrongness back at them without lowering yourself to their level with a comment like, "Wow, you just said that in front of people" or say "What do you mean?" until they either give up on you or explain their jerkish statements in a way that makes them realize how bad they sound.

If the person is harassing you...

Do not engage with them. They want a reaction. Assess the level of danger here: Have they made violent threats? Do they seem able to follow through on those threats? Would there be immediate consequences to them escalating to violence in this place? If the answer to any of those questions is yes, remove yourself from the situation calmly but quickly and get somewhere safe. If the answer is all no's, you still don't owe this person your time, attention, or excuses. Just leave.

I am not obligated to explain my gender to everyone who asks.

I will not compare myself to other people on the internet.

Internet Troll Bingo

As a trans person on the internet, at some point you are likely to be the target of trolls. Rather than respond to their hateful rhetoric or take it personally, let's make it into a game.

Bonus racism, sexism, ableism, homophobia, fatphobia, etc.	Calls you a pervert	"You need therapy"	Makes up ridiculous pronouns for themself	Thinks they're an expert in biology but they're not
Insults your looks	Inaccurate insult	"Trans people should be [terrible action here]"	Thinks gay and trans are the same thing	Calls you "it" without permission
"Corrects" someone's use of your pronoun	"I identify as an attack helicopter"	free	Confuses trans men and trans women	Thinks you care that they're not attracted to you
Fetishizes your body	Accuses you of attention seeking	Replies to selfie with "what is it?"	"What about the children?"	Repeat offender
Obligatory genital mention	"Special snowflake"	Flirty until they realize you're trans	Conservative politics in username/icon	Threat (block and report!)

Trolls tend to say many of the same things as the critical voices in your own brain (aka the Jerkbrain). When a troll comment bothers you, ask yourself: Is this something my brain is telling me, too? Remind yourself that if your Jerkbrain is saying the same things as those repugnant internet carbuncles, its judgment is not to be trusted.

CHAPTER 7
GENDER EUPHORIA

Gender euphoria is the state of comfort or joy brought on by confirming your true gender. Trans people find gender euphoria in many different ways, including presenting as our real genders, hearing others use our correct pronouns, engaging in activities that affirm our genders, and even thinking about things that make us happy about our gender identities.

Gender euphoria can be a spark of joy twirling a skirt, a moment of comfort, being called "Sir" at a restaurant, or a sense of wholeness after your name change hearing. It's different for everyone.

My favorite description of gender euphoria comes from Calvin Payne-Taylor's book *Genderbound: An Odyssey From Female to Male*: "from the moment I had voiced my trans identity that first night, every step I took felt like coming home."[9]

---

9   Calvin Payne-Taylor (2017) *Genderbound: An Odyssey from Female to Male.* Maryville, TN: Regal Crest Enterprises, p.4.

Every time I read that line, I smile. More often than not, that's what my gender euphoria feels like: Coming home.

The way you experience gender euphoria is all yours. Enjoy it.

Gender Euphoria Affirmations

Repeat the affirmations below. If writing longhand doesn't work for you, try saying them to yourself in the mirror or turning the ones you need most into a chant.

I love myself unconditionally.

I am lovable.

I am incredible.

I am gorgeous.

I will surround myself with people I love and trust.

I invite good things into my life.

I know how to bring myself joy.

_____

I am exactly where I need to be.

_____

I am in control of my thoughts and my life.

_____

I love myself and who I am.

_____

What do you need to hear to celebrate yourself? Write your own affirmations below. If you have recurring negative thoughts about your ability to feel good about your gender ("I'll never feel good about my gender"), try turning its opposite into an affirmation ("I deserve to feel good about my gender"). Keep your language positive and sincere.

_____

_____

_____

_____

_____

Draw what makes you feel at home in your gender.

I am enough exactly as I am.

When have you felt gender euphoria, big or small? What triggered it? What did it feel like in your body?

THE TRANS SELF-CARE WORKBOOK

Things that Give Me Gender Euphoria

Below is a list of things that have sparked gender euphoria for other trans people. Circle the things that work for you and add your own!

◇◇ Presenting as my correct gender

◇◇ Wearing a favorite item of clothing

◇◇ Being called "Sir" or "Ma'am" in public

◇◇ A loved one using my chosen name

◇◇ Realizing a new friend has never known me by my deadname

◇◇ Signing my chosen name on a piece of art

◇◇ Experimenting with my gender presentation

◇◇ Writing poetry about gender

◇◇ Twirling a skirt

◇◇ Beauty-related self-care like facials

◇◇ Attending a trans rights protest

◇◇ Tying a necktie

◇◇ Applying makeup

◇◇ Participating in a drag show

◇◇ Exercising and enjoying my body's strength

◇◇ Standing up for my gender identity and being listened to

◇◇ Being included in groups that exclude my gender of origin

◇◇ Using (or having someone else use) different words for my body parts

◇◇ Making a self-portrait

◇◇ Attending Pride events

◇◇ Wearing a costume

◇◇◇ Getting a gender-neutral greeting at a restaurant

◇◇◇ Participating in events as my true self

◇◇◇ _____

◇◇◇ _____

◇◇◇ _____

◇◇◇ _____

◇◇◇ _____

Things I'd Like to Try

Finding things that make you feel your best takes trial and error. Let's brainstorm some new things you can try to explore gender euphoria and just chase your own happiness!

What can you do to explore your gender euphoria? (Some suggestions from other trans folks: role-play or tabletop games, shopping with trusted friends, cosplay, writing and art, modeling, trans pool parties.)

_____

_____

_____

_____

_____

_____

_____

_____

What have you always wanted to try? It's okay to daydream.

_____

_____

_____

_____

_____

Does anything on those lists stand out as a thing you'd like to actually pursue?

I am part of this world, and I will live in it.

Many Uses for a Notebook

An empty notebook, planner, or blank book can become a helpful tool for your transition. Try one of the ideas below.

- A hormone diary: If you're going on HRT, write down changes in your body/mind as you notice them (this can also be helpful for your doctor)

- A mood tracker: Make a note of what your mood was and what you did each day. After a couple of weeks, look back and see if there's any correlation between your good moods and what you did on those days

- A sticker chart: Buy a pack of stickers that make you smile, and every time you do something difficult or do something nice for yourself, put a sticker on that day

- A bullet journal: Track whatever you want! To-do lists, charts, notes—bullet journals can be a great organizational tool, if that's what you need

- A stream of consciousness diary to get your thoughts down and then let them go

I will enjoy the good things that come into my life.

A Very Good Day Letter

Write a letter to your future self about a very good day you had where you felt most like yourself. Do your best to describe the sense of comfort, happiness, or excitement of that day. Another time, when you're feeling low, come back to this letter and re-read it.

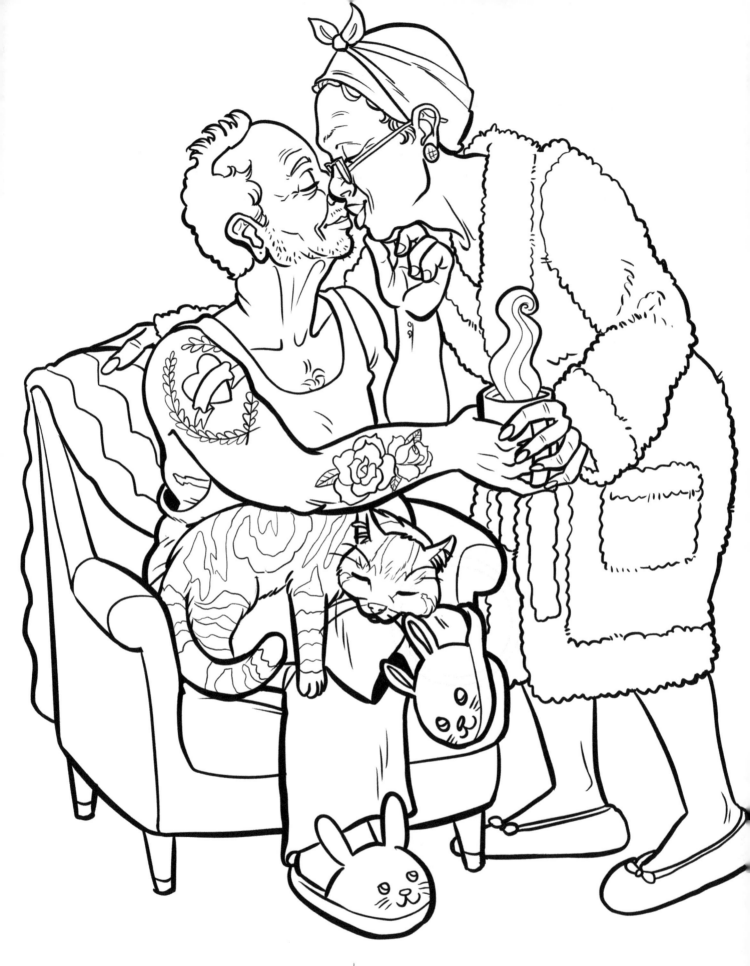

We're trans, and we're not going anywhere.

CHAPTER 8
WHEN THE GOING GETS TOUGH

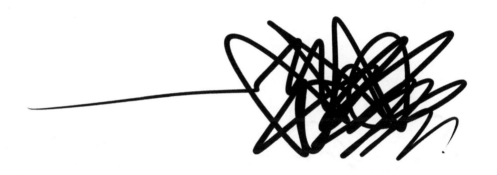

This chapter deals with heavy topics, including mental illness and suicide. If you're struggling right now, please contact one of these crisis lines for help:

Trans Lifeline: US: 877-565-8860; Canada: 877-330-6366

The Trevor Project: 866-488-7386; chat and text help: thetrevorproject.org/get-help-now

National Trans 24 Hotline (UK only): 0844 3583204 or 0752 7524034

FEELING TERRIBLE? REPLENISH YOUR BASIC NEEDS!

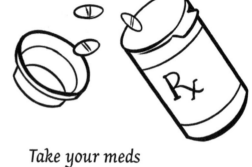

Take your meds

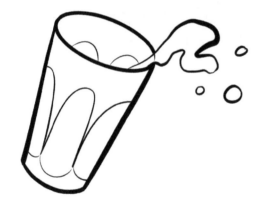

Drink water

Eat food

Take a bath or shower

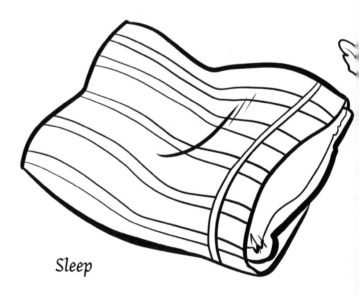

Sleep

Emergency Plan

You are lovable and you deserve to be here. This page is for you to fill out and read when you need to be reminded of that.

Write down five things that usually make you feel even a little bit better. If you're having trouble thinking of five, look back at your lists of good stuff in previous chapters.

1. _____

2. _____

3. _____

4. _____

5. _____

Write down three people who care about you and ways you can reach them when you need to talk to someone.

1. _____

2. _____

3. _____

If you're feeling down, choose one thing on this list to do. Reach out to your trusted people. These feelings will pass.

Make your own self-care merit badges!
What do you deserve credit for today?

took my hormones

showered

wrote affirmations

Identifying Your Resiliency Factors

Resiliency factors are the opposite of risk factors. Your resiliency factors are things in your life that help you cope with difficult situations.

External resiliency factors are things like community, money, or location (being in a large city with trans health resources, for example). You have little or no control over these, but use them to your advantage when you need them!

What are your external resiliency factors?

_____

_____

_____

_____

_____

_____

_____

_____

Internal resiliency factors are things you usually have some control over that come from inside, like humor, meaning finding (finding a purpose, feeling like you're helping others), confidence, hobbies you enjoy that you participate in regularly, basic self-care, creative outlets, or the ability to moderate your access to trauma (turning off the news, avoiding abusers, etc.).

What are your internal resiliency factors?

_____

_____

_____

_____

_____

_____

_____

_____

_____

When life feels difficult or you are in a traumatic situation, utilize your resiliency factors to get through it.

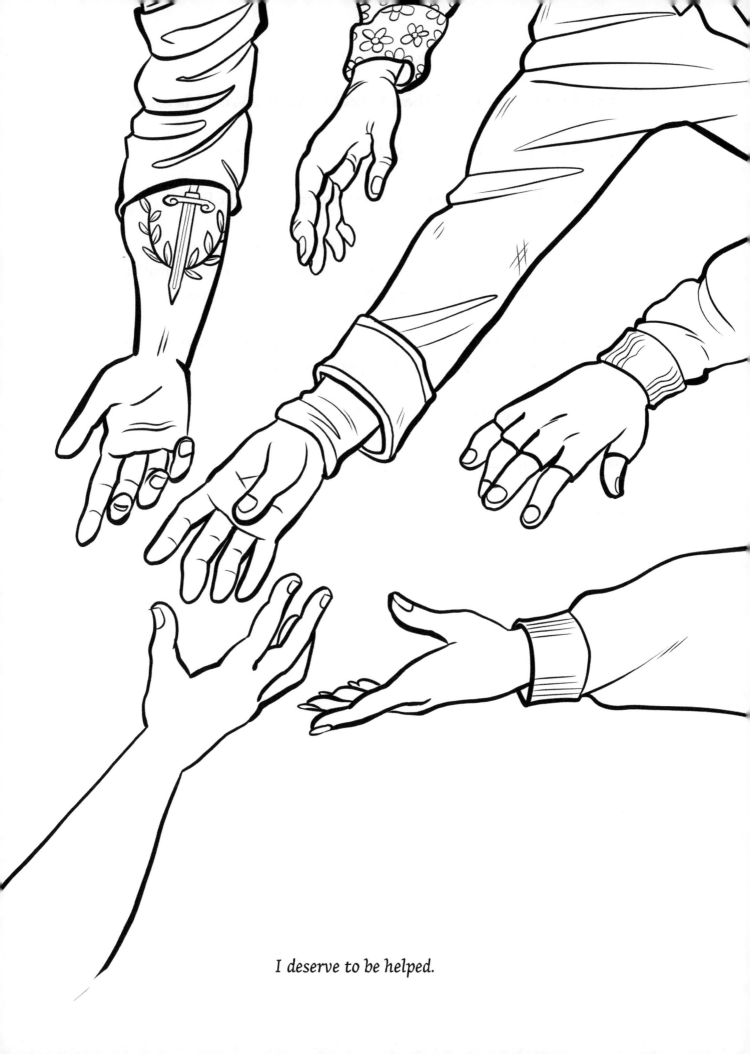

I deserve to be helped.

Why Bother Fighting When It Feels Like the World Is on Fire?

Because the world is better with you in it.

Because if you're not here, there's one less person to fight the fire.

Because to balance out the dumpster fire of misery that the world is sometimes, we have to contribute to the sum of human happiness. If you're human, that means you're on the list of humans whose happiness contributes.

Because for every one of us who's out here living our lives while trans, there's a kid in the next generation who's seeing us as role models.

Because depriving yourself of joy doesn't help anyone else.

Because there is still so much to enjoy in this world.

Because...don't you want to know what happens next?

Forgiveness Affirmations

Repeat the affirmations below. If writing longhand doesn't work for you, try saying them to yourself in the mirror or turning the ones you need most into a chant.

I forgive myself for not asserting my pronouns when I was nervous.

I forgive myself for not coming out sooner.

I forgive myself for not knowing who I was.

I forgive myself for not knowing what I needed.

I forgive myself for not always being who I wanted to be.

I forgive myself for the things I did when I didn't like my body.

I forgive myself for being afraid.

I forgive myself for being just as vulnerable and human as everyone else.

I forgive my brain for not always being kind to me.

_____

I forgive my body for not always being what I needed.

_____

What do you need to forgive yourself for? Write your own affirmations below. If you have recurring thoughts of guilt or shame ("I haven't done my best for the people I love"), try turning it into a forgiveness affirmation ("I forgive myself for not always being there for the people I love"). Keep your language positive and sincere.

_____

_____

_____

_____

_____

Affirmations for Low Moments

I deserve to be here.

The world is a better place with me in it.

This pain will pass.

I will get through this.

Everything in life can change, including these feelings.

I don't need to be perfect.

I am loved.

I am needed.

I am important.

What do you need to hear to keep you going right now? Write your own affirmations below. If you have recurring negative thoughts ("I can't survive this"), try turning its opposite into an affirmation ("I am a survivor"). Keep your language positive and sincere.

Finding What Helps You

What do you wish someone would tell you when you're feeling low?

_____

_____

_____

_____

_____

_____

_____

What would you tell a friend who's feeling this way?

_____

_____

_____

_____

_____

_____

_____

_____

Write a letter to your past self telling them about the good things you've gotten to do because they stuck around. Be kind to your past self; you know what you were going through.

Write an encouraging letter to your future self for when you feel down. Come back to read it when you need it.

Make a Compliment Box

You will need

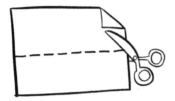

Paper

Scissors

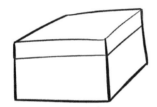

A box with a lid

Writing implements

This is best done as a gift. Make one for a friend, or ask a loved one to make one for you!

Reach out to loved ones of the person the box is for and ask them to tell you a few things they love about that person. Write those compliments down on strips of paper (or type them up, print them out, and cut the page up). Put those compliment strips into the box and give it to the person who needs it.

When they're feeling low or unworthy, now they have a physical reminder of why people love them.

Stuff to Stick Around for

Sometimes the little things are enough to keep you kicking.

Write down three things you're excited about.

_____

_____

_____

Write about three things you're curious to learn more about.

_____

_____

_____

Write about three things you'd like to do—big or small—in the next year.

_____

_____

_____

Write the names of three people you'd like to spend time with soon.

_____

_____

_____

I will outlive this and I will thrive.

Color the shapes with the dots to reveal a hidden message.

CHAPTER 9
SOCIAL MOVEMENTS

Surviving the Trans Rights Debate

We're living in a period of trans history where our rights are disputed in courts, on the news, and all across social media. Dealing with that reality takes a toll on us. It is a stressor at the very least, and for many of us it's trauma.

This chapter talks a lot about fighting for change. That's one way that people react to living in world that's hostile to their existence, and it's the way I react personally, but I want to make something very clear: You don't have to do this unless you want to.

You are not required to be a warrior. You have no obligation to fight for yourself and others, to hold a sign and march in the cold, or to give your money to non-profits. You don't even have to vote if you don't want to. (But please vote anyway.)

There's nothing wrong with avoiding emotionally dangerous confrontations, staying in during protests, and using that last $10 to order yourself a sandwich.

There are many ways to make the world a better place.

If you want to fight for our rights, fight.

If you want to assist those who fight, assist.

If you want to contribute on a small scale, contribute.

And if you don't want to do any of that, or if the trauma is too much to handle, or if you just need a damn break, take care of yourself. You are part of this world, so taking care of you makes the world a better place, too.

I'm making the world a better place just by being myself.

Learning and Listening

To make the world a better place for ourselves and for the people we love, we need to know how to listen to each other. Change requires learning, and learning new things means understanding that you're not always right. This process can hurt—trust me, I feel you. As a white person who grew up in an aggressively white, middle-class, nuclear family-filled suburb, I've had to come to terms with my own wrongness a lot. You'll get through it.

You will find that your own stances on things have become outdated, or that you didn't have all the facts when you developed a belief, or that you have been speaking over people with less privilege than yourself. Don't go into a guilt spiral—listen to your guilt and use it as motivation to improve. The important thing is that you pause, listen, and learn.

Learning can be uncomfortable. You might feel defensive or ashamed. That's because learning is a constant cycle of accepting change, which is hard for humans. On the plus side, your brain has a predictable path to accepting change, and once you know it, you can more easily identify what state you're at and move on.

You might have heard about the five stages of grief named by Elisabeth Kübler-Ross: Denial, Anger, Bargaining, Depression, and Acceptance. Well, the cycle of acceptance of change—the process by which we learn we were wrong—is very similar.

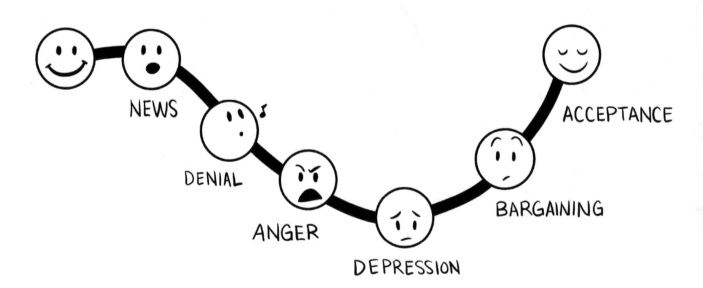

CYCLE of ACCEPTANCE

NEWS

DENIAL

ANGER

DEPRESSION

BARGAINING

ACCEPTANCE

If you're reading this book you're probably a human, so this is a cycle you can expect to see your brain go through whenever you learn something that challenges you. It might take your brain five seconds or five months to go through the whole cycle, and the length of various stages will vary. You might repeat stages. This is not an exact map of your internal process, just a general framework to help you figure out where you're at.

Learning is change, and change can be hard. Be patient with yourself.

Write about a core value that is close to your heart (such as justice, empathy, or family). What moment(s) in your life made you realize how important it is to you? How does this value affect the way you live your life?

Making Changes on a Small Scale

Start small! Showing love to your local community, your home, and yourself is important. Here are some ideas to get started. Add your own below.

- Writing fiction that features trans people

- Making art that features trans people

- Doing self-care activities with my loved ones

- Decorating my community space

- Participating in a community garden

- Voting in local elections

- Making art (any kind) to share with my online or IRL community

- Being out in public/online

- Putting cute photos of my pets on social media to interrupt difficult news days

- Inviting friends who are stressed out to cuddle my pets

- Cleaning my home, neighborhood, or local park

- Encouraging myself and my trans friends to avoid anti-trans accounts online (purposely reading hurtful things can be a form of self-harm)

- Nourishing my community by planning, hosting, or contributing to trans-friendly social events

- Taking care of community animals (making birdhouses/bathouses/ winter cat shelters, getting involved in trap, neuter, release programs, planting bee- and butterfly-friendly flowers)

- Talking openly about people in my community who've shown their transphobic/homophobic/racist/abelist/etc. sides and not inviting them to things. Holding them accountable

🌰 Contributing to clothing drives for homeless shelters and women's shelters (socks and menstrual products are relatively inexpensive and always needed)

🌰 _____

🌰 _____

🌰 _____

🌰 _____

🌰 _____

Making Political Changes

Voting is the most direct way to create political change, and protesting is the most visible. Here are some little ways you can make big changes happen.

 Vote on Election Day and encourage the people you care about to do the same

 Call or email your elected officials to stand up for causes you support. If you're nervous about talking on the phone, call after business hours when no one is in the office, and leave a message. You can find your representative's contact information on their government profiles, or on sites like 5Calls.org (USA) that also supply scripts for you to follow

 Donate money to the campaigns of candidates you support

 Volunteer for candidates you support (especially if you're comfortable with phone calls or door-knocking, but there are all sorts of jobs to do!)

 Get involved in the polls—your local polling place needs volunteers to staff it on Election Day

 Talk about the elections with friends and family to help them understand why voting is important

 Protest! Look for local protests online

 If you want to protest but can't because of disability, childcare concerns, scheduling, anxiety, or other reasons, you can always help in other ways, like driving friends who are protesting to or from the event, making signs, and helping them free up their time by babysitting or picking up work shifts

 Promote protests and pro-trans events on social media

 Donate to the cause, including: charities, legal funds, funds for people directly affected, and bail funds for protesters

My anger is valuable.

What makes you excited about your social movement? What makes you proud to be a part of it? What does progress feel like to you?

_____

_____

_____

_____

_____

_____

_____

_____

_____

Identifying and Avoiding Burnout

While engaging in activism—especially activism to defend our own rights, which is emotionally draining—it's important to identify the point where you need to take a break. You're not a superhero, even if you do look fabulous in tights. Taking breaks periodically will help you fight the good fight longer and not burn out.

Burnout is a state of being in such constant stress that you exhaust yourself emotionally and physically. It usually involves feelings of detachment from things you used to care about, a sense that your work is suffering, and cynicism replacing hopefulness.

Have you ever burned out before (at activism, work, art, etc.)? What did it feel like? What made you realize you were burned out?

_____

What warning signs from that experience could you watch for in the future? (Common signs of burnout include increased apathy, depression and anxiety, chronic fatigue, getting sick more often, lack of focus, and irritability.)

When you're experiencing burnout, it can be difficult to remember that you're capable of doing good things. If you're feeling burned out right now, use this space to write a list of things you've done in the past six months or a year, along with the good things that have come from those actions.

You can also return to your "Caring for Yourself" list in Chapter 2 for ideas on how to treat yourself kindly during this time.

Social Movement Affirmations

Repeat the affirmations below. If writing longhand doesn't work for you, try saying them to yourself in the mirror or turning the ones you need most into a chant.

I have the power to create change.

I am one of many.

I am committed to progress.

Taking care of myself helps me take care of others.

I am making the world a better place just by being myself.

I don't need to be a warrior all the time.

I am resilient.

It's okay for me to change my mind.

It's okay if I'm wrong.

_____

I am secure enough to open my heart and listen to others.

_____

What do you need to hear on this subject? Write your own affirmations below. If you have recurring negative thoughts about your place in social movements ("I'm not doing enough to help"), try turning its opposite into an affirmation ("I'm doing my best to help"). Keep your language positive and sincere.

_____

_____

_____

_____

_____

Even dumpster fires burn out eventually.

Afterword

When I started writing this book, I thought I was done with my own transition. I had gotten my legal name change, had top surgery, changed my pronouns to they/them, and come out in so many areas of my life that the first time my plumber called me "ma'am" I briefly thought, "I should come out to him so he doesn't feel left out." (I have not, as of this writing, come out to my plumber. Paul, if you're reading this, hey...)

Everything about my gender felt settled, *finally*.

And then I started working on this book, and I started, inadvertently, doing the exercises in my head as I wrote them down. I became passionate about affirmations and started writing my own. I drew over four-dozen happy trans people.

And then I started swearing, because this fucking book therapized me into realizing that my transition isn't done. I hadn't allowed myself to even consider the option in years, but dammit, I think I want to go on HRT.

I am still not done swearing at this book. Apparently, I'm also not done becoming the person I want to present to the world. By the time this book is in your hands, I don't know where I'll be at in my transition. I don't know for sure whether I'll be on testosterone or not.

That's okay.

I don't need to be a finished project. Few people are.

You don't need to be finished either. It's okay to be wherever you are.

Whoever we are right now, we deserve the world.

Acknowledgements

This book would not exist without the support of the following incredible people:

My family, Peregrin, Quin, and Lexi, who provided unyielding love and support throughout this project, even when I was insufferably anxious.

Teri Blauersouth, MA, LPCC, who guided this book in a more therapeutic direction with their candid consultation and brainstorming sessions over pie.

Kerry Edna MacDonald, LICSW, who provided a valuable second opinion on the book and reminded me to sleep.

Ty Blauersouth, my go-to beta reader, for saying, "This book doesn't sound like you" and prompting a total rewrite six weeks before deadline. It's better now.

The Wyrdsmiths, my very patient writers group, who read the whole thing in three days even though there aren't any dragons in it. To Naomi Kritzer, Lyda Morehouse, Adam Stemple, Kelly Barnhill, and Eleanor Arnason: I owe you coffee.

All the friends who have given me feedback, been my accountabilibuddies while making art, and supported me with distant cheering and healthy boundaries while I was a deadline hermit.

And, of course, I owe my thanks to my incredible agent Naomi Davis, who fought for this book to exist, and my editor Andrew James, who believed enough in this book and in me to let me run amok with it.

Thank you, thank you, thank you.

Trans Love

An Anthology of Transgender and
Non-Binary Voices
Edited by Freiya Benson

£14.99 | $19.95 | PB | 296PP | ISBN-978 1 78592 432 3
EISBN-978 1 78450 804 3

**Selected as a 2019 LGBT Book of the
Year by Dazed and Ms. Magazine.**

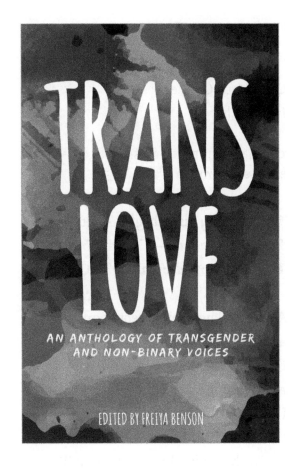

A ground-breaking anthology of
writing on the topic of love, written
by trans and non-binary people
who share their thoughts, feelings,
and experiences of love in all its
guises. The collection spans familial,
romantic, spiritual, and self-love as
well as friendships and ally love, to provide a broad and honest understanding
of how trans people navigate love and relationships, and what love means
to them.

Reclaiming what love means to trans people, this book provokes
conversations that are not reflected in what is presently written, moving the
narrative around trans identities away from sensationalism. At once intimate
and radical, and both humorous and poignant, this book is for anyone who
has loved, who is in love, and who is looking for love.

Freiya Benson is a trans woman and an experienced writer, and has written for magazines
and websites, including the *Huffington Post* and *Vice*.

Trans Power

Own Your Gender
Juno Roche

£12.99 | $18.95 | PB | 256PP | ISBN-978 1 78775 019 7
EISBN-978 1 78775 020 3

"Staggeringly visionary"—Attitude
"Essential reading"—Charlie Craggs
"Bold and ground-breaking"—Owl

"All those layers of expectation that are thrust upon us; boy, masculine, femme, transgender, sexual, woman, real, are such a weight to carry round. I feel transgressive. I feel hybrid. I feel trans."

In this radical and emotionally raw book, Juno Roche pushes the boundaries of trans representation by redefining "trans" as an identity with its own power and strength that goes beyond the gender binary.

Through intimate conversations with leading and influential figures in the trans community, such as Kate Bornstein, Travis Alabanza, Josephine Jones, Glamrou, and E-J Scott, this book highlights the diversity of trans identities and experiences with regard to love, bodies, sex, race, and class, and urges trans people—and the world at large—to embrace a "trans" identity as something that offers empowerment and autonomy.

Powerfully written, and with humor and advice throughout, this book is essential reading for anyone interested in the future of gender and how we identify ourselves.

Juno Roche is an internationally recognized trans writer and campaigner, and Founder of Trans Workers UK and the Trans Teachers Network. On the Independent's Rainbow List 2015 and 2016, they are a patron of cliniQ and received the 2015 NUT Blair Peach Award for the campaign "Why Trans Teachers Matter." They regularly contribute to publications including *Diva*, *The Guardian*, and *Vice* and is the author of *Queer Sex* (Longlisted for the Polari First Book Prize).

How to Understand Your Gender

A Practical Guide for Exploring
Who You Are
Alex Iantaffi and Meg-John Barker
Foreword by S. Bear Bergman

£14.99 | $19.95 | PB | 288PP | ISBN-978 1 78592 746 1
EISBN-978 1 78450 517 2

"For anyone who's ever wished they had a smart, kind, friend with whom they could calmly and safely discuss gender issues: this most excellent book is that kind of friend."—Kate Bornstein, author of *Gender Outlaw*

Have you ever questioned your own gender identity? Do you know somebody who is transgender or who identifies as non-binary? Do you ever feel confused when people talk about gender diversity?

This down-to-earth guide is for anybody who wants to know more about gender, from its biology, history, and sociology, to how it plays a role in our relationships and interactions with family, friends, partners, and strangers. It looks at practical ways people can express their own gender, and will help you to understand people whose gender might be different from your own. With activities and points for reflection throughout, this book will help people of all genders engage with gender diversity and explore the ideas in the book in relation to their own lived experiences.

Alex Iantaffi is a licensed marriage and family therapist, supervisor, sex therapist, scholar, and Editor-in-Chief of the *Journal of Sexual and Relationship Therapy*. He is also adjunct faculty at the University of Wisconsin-Stout, a parent, and active community organizer. @xtaffi on Twitter.

Meg-John Barker is a writer, therapist, and activist-academic specializing in sex, gender, and relationships. They are a senior lecturer in psychology at the Open University. @megjohnbarker on Twitter.